The East African Slave Trade: The History and Legacy of the Arab Slave Trade and the Indian Ocean Slave Trade

By Charles River Editors

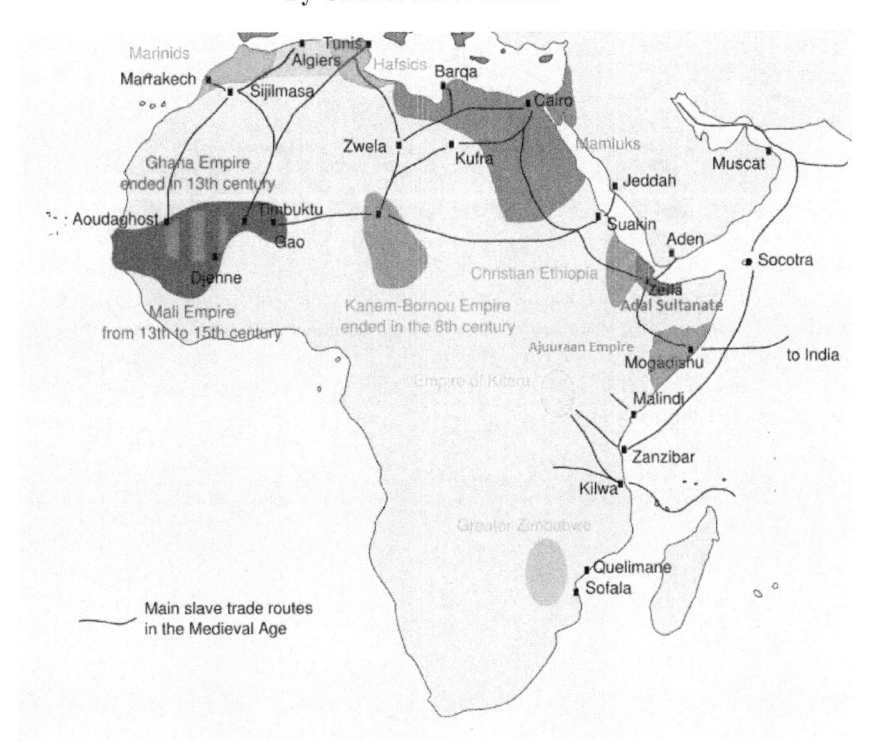

A map of African slave trade routes

About Charles River Editors

Charles River Editors provides superior editing and original writing services across the digital publishing industry, with the expertise to create digital content for publishers across a vast range of subject matter. In addition to providing original digital content for third party publishers, we also republish civilization's greatest literary works, bringing them to new generations of readers via ebooks.

Sign up here to receive updates about free books as we publish them, and visit Our Kindle Author Page to browse today's free promotions and our most recently published Kindle titles.

Introduction

"The Slave Trade" by Auguste François Biard (1840)

The East African Slave Trade

"It is certain that large numbers of slaves were exported from eastern Africa; the best evidence for this is the magnitude of the Zanj revolt in Iraq in the 9th century, though not all of the slaves involved were Zanj. There is little evidence of what part of eastern Africa the Zanj came from, for the name is here evidently used in its general sense, rather than to designate the particular stretch of the coast, from about 3°N. to 5°S., to which the name was also applied." - Ghada Hashem Talhami "The Zanj Rebellion Reconsidered". *The International Journal of African Historical Studies*. 10 (3): 443–461. (1977).

It has often been said that the greatest invention of all time was the sail, which facilitated the internationalization of the globe and thus ushered in the modern era. Columbus' contact with the New World, alongside European maritime contact with the Far East, transformed human history, and in particular the history of Africa. It was the sail that linked the continents of Africa, Asia, and Europe, and thus it was also the sail that facilitated the greatest involuntary human migration of all time.

The Transatlantic Slave Trade was founded by the Portuguese in the 15th century for the specific purpose of supplying the New World colonies with African slave labor. It was soon joined by all the major trading powers of Europe, and it reached its peak in the 18th century with the founding and development of plantation economies that ran from the South American mainland through the Caribbean and into the southern states of the United States. Toward the end of the 18th century, it began to fall into decline, and by the beginning of the 19th century, various abolition movements heralded its eventual outlawing. It was, throughout its existence, however, a purely commercial phenomenon, supplying agricultural power to vast plantations on an industrial scale. In every respect, it was unaffected and uninfluenced by history, sentimentality, tradition, or common law. Slaves transported across the Atlantic Ocean remained a commodity with a codified value, like a horse or a steam engine, existing often within an equation of obsolescence and replacement that was cheaper than nurturing and maintenance.

The East African Slave Trade on the other hand, or the Indian Ocean Slave Trade as it was also known, was a far more complex and nuanced phenomenon, far older, significantly more widespread, rooted in ancient traditions, and governed by rules very different to those in the western hemisphere. It is also often referred to as the Arab Slave Trade, although this, specifically, might perhaps be more accurately applied to the more ancient variant of organized African slavery, affecting North Africa, and undertaken prior to the advent of Islam and certainly prior to the spread of the institution south as far as the south/east African coast. It also involved the slavery of non-African races and was, therefore, more general in scope.

The African slave trade is a complex and deeply divisive subject that has had a tendency to evolve according the political requirements of any given age, and is often touchable only with the correct distribution of culpability. It has for many years, therefore, been deemed singularly unpalatable to implicate Africans themselves in the perpetration of the institution, and only in recent years has the large-scale African involvement in both the Atlantic and Indian Ocean Slave Trades come to be an accepted fact. There can, however, be no doubt that even though large numbers of indigenous Africans were liable, it was European ingenuity and greed that fundamentally drove the industrialization of the Transatlantic slave trade in response to massive new market demands created by their equally ruthless exploitation of the Americas.

The East African Slave Trade: The History and Legacy of the Arab Slave Trade and the Indian Ocean Slave Trade examines the turbulent history of slavery across Africa and the consequences it has had. Along with pictures of important people, places, and events, you will learn about the East African Slave Trade like never before.

The East African Slave Trade: The History and Legacy of the Arab Slave Trade and the Indian Ocean Slave Trade

About Charles River Editors

Introduction

   The Indian Ocean Slave Trade

   The Universities Mission to Central Africa

   The Beginning of the End

   Abolition

   Online Resources

   Further Reading

Free Books by Charles River Editors

Discounted Books by Charles River Editors

The Indian Ocean Slave Trade

"The Calipha in Baghdad at the beginning of the 10th Century had 7,000 black eunuchs and 4,000 white eunuchs in his palace." – Ronald Segal, *Islam's Black Slaves: The Other Black Diaspora*

In 1841, a young Scottish missionary doctor of the London Missionary Society arrived in Cape Town, commencing one of the most extraordinary careers in exploration and missionary work ever recorded on the continent of Africa. David Livingstone was born in 1813 to the family of an itinerate tea seller, and his early years were passed in a condition of child labor in a Scottish cotton gin. He provided largely for his own education in the little spare time that he had, eventually graduating from the University of Glasgow with a degree in Medicine. He was a man of titanic faith, and his vocation from a very early age was to serve as a foreign missionary. This was the age of European global expansion, driven by rapid advances in technology, industry, and science, and it was an age led in many areas by the British. By the end of the century, most of the known world had fallen under some form of European control, and much of the early pioneering work to achieving this had been done by missionaries.

Livingstone's initial objective had been to serve on behalf of the London Missionary Society in China, but the outbreak of the first Opium War in 1839 frustrated this, and for a while, he considered America or the West Indies. Then, by chance, he met the celebrated Scottish missionary Robert Moffat while visiting London from South Africa, and it was Moffat who persuaded Livingstone to make his career in Africa. He was a man in his mid-forties, and the established doyen of the southern African missionary movement, where he ruled from his station of Kuruman in the Karoo region of what is today the Northern Cape.

Livingstone

Moffat

Moffat would soon discover, however, that his new protégé, at 28-years old, was an individualistic, idiosyncratic character, uneasy under the management of any other and unhappy under conditions of humble, settled missionary labor. He yearned to carry forward his ministry into the sparsely explored hinterland of the northern interior, and after months of agitation, he finally secured permission from the board of the London Missionary Society to do so. Throughout his life, Livingstone would maintain that his chief vocation remained always his missionary work and his service to God, but his wandering nature and his urge to explore consistently got the better of him, and it is, quite justly, as an explorer that he is better recognized today.

Nonetheless, his faith would remain consistent throughout his life, and it would inform every aspect of his exploration. Livingstone was a humanitarian, and through his travels, he bore consistent witness to the unfolding horror of the slave trade in south/central Africa, and he labored unceasingly toward its eradication. As he probed incrementally northward through modern-day Botswana, he eventually arrived in the region of the Zambezi River that is concurrent broadly with the confluence of the modern borders of Zimbabwe, Botswana, Zambia, and Namibia. Here he began to encounter the first direct evidence of slave activity, originating from the Portuguese territory of West Africa, later to become Angola. This was to supply rogue Portuguese traders at the coast, under a tolerant metropolitan regime, and it involved a handful of powerful local tribes in various parts of the hinterland in the acquisition and sale of slaves.

Observing this, Livingstone began to consider a solution, and in due course, he came up with what he called Christianity and Commerce. By the mid-1850s, at the time that this was taking place, the trade in slaves by the European trading nations had generally been outlawed, and a British naval blockade sought to enforce this ban in the Atlantic and along much of the West African coast. Portuguese slave traders, however, kept up an illicit trade in all its African territories, and the practical effects of this were what Livingstone encountered when he reached the Zambezi. He contacted local leaders and urged them to desist and embrace Christianity, but while he could preach, his words, in the end, had very insignificant, if any, effect at all.

The essence of his concept of Christianity and Commerce, however, was quite simple. The introduction of Anglo-Saxon Christian values would instill in a pagan race the simple virtues of humanity and humility, while commerce would introduce alternative avenues for powerful and wealthy local leaders to acquire and retain wealth other than through the capture and sale of one another. Central to this strategy would, of course, be a viable highway into the interior. When Livingstone finally arrived on the south bank of the great Zambezi River, he felt certain that this was precisely what he had found.

What thereafter followed was one of the great epics of African exploration. The year was 1853, and Livingstone stood at the site of that monumental natural spectacle that he would later name Victoria Falls, situated equidistant between the west and east African coasts. He decided first to attempt an exploration upstream, in the direction of Portuguese West Africa (Angola), perhaps in respect of the fact that the west coast lay closer to Europe. However, after months of punishing travel, he arrived in the Portuguese port settlement of Loanda and was forced to conclude that this route did not represent a viable highway into the interior. After a brief sojourn with his Portuguese hosts, he returned from whence he had come, and thereafter, he began an exploration of the Zambezi River in an easterly direction, downstream toward the Indian Ocean, and in every respect, this offered a more promising prospect.

A month or two later, as he neared the coast, he allowed himself for the first time to believe that this was indeed God's highway to the interior, and anxious now to get to the coast, he transected a wide bend in the river, making his way directly to the Portuguese port of Quelimane. There, the news of what he had achieved broke, and he was greeted on his return to England as a national hero. In his humble and self-effacing way, Livingstone had bested the greatest explorers of the age by transecting the African continent on foot from west to east.

The sudden and unexpected celebrity that this brought did not impress Livingstone, other than to offer this otherwise unimportant missionary a voice and influence that he otherwise would never have had, and launched, arguably, the first dedicated humanitarian career of the modern age. His message to the Victorian public was simply that the obscurity of Africa, the last great unclaimed quarter of the world, hid an unfolding humanitarian crisis that was the obligation of Great Britain, the most powerful nation in the world, to address. The organized slave trade, outlawed by then by all the major powers of Europe and already a significant factor in the secession debate in the United States, remained very much alive in Africa.

By then, the growth of European imperialism had begun spreading to touch every continent of the world, although not yet, to quite the same degree, in Africa. European spheres of influence existed at various points along the coast of Africa, mainly as a residue of the Atlantic Slave Trade, but no comprehensive effort so far had been made at European colonization. The interior of the continent remained very much terra incognita, isolated by challenging geography, tropical disease, and the perception that Africa had little other than its own people to offer, and upon the abolition of slavery and the end of that trade, the attention of the European capital element began to drift elsewhere. Africa, apart from the long-held colonies and republics of the extreme south, was left to the missionaries and the explorers.

Livingstone, of course, was both, but his professional concern did not necessarily reflect those of other great explorers of the age, such as those who determined the Northwest Passage, for example, or explored the continental United States, or circumnavigated Australia. These were geographic and imperial projects, undertaken by Royal Navy men or scientists and geographers, often in pursuit of career or financial or social advancement. Livingstone was among the first to attempt a definition of imperialism as moral, underwritten by an obligation on the part of the civilized races to nurture, protect, and uplift the savage and as a God-given mission to advance and civilize the pagan reaches of the world.

As he toured Britain in the spring and summer of 1857, publishing and lecturing widely to a rapt public, Livingstone's homily remained unchanged, and it fell on very fertile ground. The Victorian public responded to this idea. With great power, there came great responsibility, and since philanthropy is the prerogative of the wealthy, it befitted a nation such as Britain, on the cusp of the greatest empire known to man, to display its great power in the world by using that power to benefit the uncivilized races now falling subject to British protection.

To achieve this, Livingstone offered his audiences a solid proposal. He had determined that the Zambezi River was navigable from its delta to the base of the Victoria Falls, and this, he repeatedly assured his listeners, was the necessary highway into the interior. What remained was simply for the British public to provide the moral and financial support for him to return to Africa and establish that highway as a means for Commerce and Christianity to be introduced to the pagan masses of the interior and save them from themselves.

In due course, Livingstone was granted his public subscription, and in 1858, he set off back to Africa at the head of a lavish expedition, the Zambezi Expedition, supported by a technical and academic staff and an impressive compliment of publicly funded materiel. The expedition was extravagant and hailed in the press as the advance guard of British moral leadership in the world and the vanguard of Christianity and Commerce, and not for a moment did Doctor David Livingstone, nor the great British public, doubt it.

Behind the scenes, however, a quieter and perhaps more considered missionary response was taking place. The Universities of Oxford, Cambridge, and Durham founded what came to be known as the Universities Mission to Central Africa, the instrument that would furnish the spiritual bedrock of Livingstone's great civilizing mission. As the hero of the expedition sailed south on the HMS *Pearl*, armed with the good wishes of the nation to forge that passage into the African interior, the UMCA prepared itself to follow in its wake and seed the pastoral missions upon which the entire enterprise was founded.

Since time immemorial, slavery has been integral to Arab society, and in some instances, it still is. In cases where ancient Arabic ideals are under revision, within, for example, the conventions of the West Africa Boko Haram movement or the Islamic State of Iraq and the Levant (ISIL or ISIS), what is described as Chattel Slavery, or the direct ownership of one individual by another based generally on religious exclusivity, survives under the terms of Islam. Thus, in this regard, organized slavery in the eastern hemisphere vastly predates any similarly organized slavery in the West, and statistically, the East African and Arabic branches of slavery by far exceeded the numbers of slaves exported to the New World (although, of course, such numbers will by necessity always be speculative). One question mark, in particular, has long hovered over East African statistics, and this was wastage that occurred because of rigorous methods and styles of capture and transportation and the preference often for castrated youth rather than viable males, which resulted in a brutal death toll, all of which, in combination, impacted East Africa perhaps more than West Africa during its period of greatest exploitation.

What might be regarded as the East African Slave Trade began with the exploitation of Bantu peoples settled in and acquired for slavery from the shores of Somali by Arab traders from southern Arabia, particularly from in and around Yemen. This, however, is nowadays something of a subtext to a later and much wider spread of slave trading that took place along what is today regarded as the Swahili Coast. This region stretches from the southern coast of Somalia to the north coast of modern Mozambique, encompassing the island systems of Lamu, Pemba, and Zanzibar, including the adjacent interior. The scope of the Swahili language as it is spoken today, as a common medium of communication, stretches across the entirety of Kenya, Tanzania, Rwanda, Burundi, and much of eastern Congo, touching the northern and southern coasts respectively of Mozambique and Somalia. This attests to the scope of Swahili trade in the interior — the extent to which it influenced cultural development and the extended period during which it flourished.

A 19th century picture of a Bantu slave

The character of slavery in this region — and slavery was the second major cornerstone of coastal trade, and always closely intertwined with the much more important ivory trade — was twofold. Initially, and very generally speaking, slaves were purchased or captured in the interior by coastal traders for the primary purpose of portaging ivory and other goods from the interior to the coast and only thereafter repurposed as an ancillary product for onward sale. Despite this, the trade was lucrative, and it was widespread, and from about the 9th century onward, significant numbers of indigenous Africans were finding their way to the mainland of Arabia and the Persian Gulf.

One of the first textual records of this was in contemporary reports of the Zanj Rebellion, a slave uprising that took place between 869 and 883 CE. The word Zanj was a general umbrella term used by Arabs to define the black African or Bantu races of Africa that comprised by far the greatest number of slaves present in Arabia. The Zanj Rebellion was ostensibly a slave uprising, but it also included many black freemen, and it began not far from the present-day city of Basra in modern Iraq. This was the center of an agricultural economy that, at the time, absorbed large numbers of African slaves, and the rebellion is recorded as being one of the bloodiest and most brutal in western Asian history, which lends it some perspective. It does, however, also serve to date the point at which East African Bantu slaves began to appear in significant numbers in that quarter of Arabia and the Persian Gulf.

Most of these slaves, however, probably originated in the Horn of Africa and not so much in East Africa, and this is supported by a comprehensive series of historic records documenting the movement and sale of slaves out of this region. The port town of Zayla, for example, situated on the north coast of modern Somaliland, was a major regional trading entrepôt, and it was home to one of largest regional slave markets of the ancient world, supplying Yemen with slaves from the Ethiopian Highlands and southern Sudan. Between the 10th and 16th centuries, the presence of Zanj slaves was increasingly documented across the more westerly reaches of the Arabian Peninsula and the Persian Gulf, with smaller numbers appearing in India and China. The origins of these slave populations must necessarily be obscure, thanks to the general scope of the word 'Zanj', but it can reasonably be supposed that the majority originated in the Horn of Africa and southern Sudan, with perhaps small numbers traded along the Swahili Coast.

The first authoritative mention of Arabian-bound Zanj slaves originating south of the Somali coast can be found in the 10th century chronicles of Buzurg ibn Shahriyar, an Islamic traveler, sailor, cartographer, and geographer who produced a collection of narratives drawn from widely dispersed Arab maritime sources of the period. Here the first mention is made of slaves originating from the area between Zanzibar and Sofala, the latter located close to the modern-day Mozambican port of Beira. The celebrated Islamic geographer Ibn Battuta makes a note in 1331 of African slaves being present at the coastal trade depot of Kilwa. This and numerous other anecdotal observations of slave activity along this coast that pop up here and there tend to suggest that commercial slave trading only began along the east coast of Africa toward the end of the 14th and during the early decades of the 15th century. By the end of the 15th century, however, the trade in slaves was well established along the entire Swahili Coast and had become a factor of everyday life and trade.

Depiction of a 13th century slave market in Africa

The Indian Ocean trade zone of the 15th and 16th centuries was a complex and interconnected network of trade routes and trade centers that followed the rim of the Indian Ocean from Madagascar to the Red Sea and from the Gulf of Aden along the southern coast of Arabia, the Persian Gulf, and the west coast of India, stretching from there to Southeast Asia and China. Between November and February, the monsoon winds from the Indian subcontinent swept across the expanse of the Indian Ocean, returning between April and September. This made possible a predictable cycle of movement for simple sailing craft plying the shore between the east coast of Africa and subcontinents of Arabia and India. The trade that developed, in consequence, was varied, but typically involved the export of raw material from Africa in the form of ivory and other wildlife products — for example, hides and Rhinoceros horn, honey and beeswax, exotic timbers, gold. Slaves seldom if ever represented a dedicated cargo, and rarely was the trade in slaves of greater value than the trade in general.

Inevitably, a degree of social interchange took place at the point of contact, and in this case, the point of contact was the East African coast. Here, Arabic-speaking settlers arrived, and a hybrid people developed, speaking a lingua franca of Arabic and Bantu, soon to be called Swahili, and gradually acculturating to Islamic religion, manners, and dress. These were and are the Swahili people, a name derived from the Arabic word Sawahil, or Coast, implying a coastal people or a language of the coast. The Swahili are an African people, but in origin and appearance they are unique and at times quite variated amongst themselves. Intermarriage with Arabs at the earliest point of contact began to produce features somewhat sharper and more Semitic and skin tones softer, and as Islam spread, dress codes and social expressions began increasingly to favor the Arabic influence.

What these coastal people, however, most gained from their exposure to the Arabs in their midst was an aptitude for trade, and as such they evolved to occupy the space of middlemen between the vast reaches of the interior and the visiting traders at the coast. In due course, as the nation defined itself, Swahili traders began to spread beyond the coast and to ply their own international trade, although for the most part they remained in the capacity of coastal traders, generating enormous wealth and subdividing into city-states positioned at various points along the coast that gave them control of the interior trade routes.

The Swahili were deeply implicated in the slave trade from the moment of its inception, although, again, never as a primary trade interest, but always as a very important and lucrative secondary enterprise. Initially, slaves were acquired for local agricultural labor within a domestic agricultural and plantation economy. Interestingly, the principal source of slaves at this point was northern Madagascar, facilitated by a similar settlement of Arabs occurring at much the same time as those on the Swahili Coast and with much the same basic effect. An Arabized indigenous society, loyal to Islam, facilitated the enslavement of local tribesmen, many of whom were then factored through the Comoros Islands, also a predominately Islamic assimilated society. Those Arabs visiting Madagascar and Comoros tended to originate from the Red Sea ports, and they took on board a small number of slaves. By far the majority were purchased by Swahili traders and transported to the mainland coast or to the islands of Pemba and Zanzibar, where conditions were fertile and large plantations were beginning to appear.

A third player in the development of the East African Slave Trade was the Portuguese. The Portuguese were the senior European colonizing power in Africa, and their entrance into the Indian Ocean trade zone can be traced to 1449, when the first Portuguese maritime contacts were established with India. By the dawn of the 16th century, a handful of Portuguese forts had been established up the coast, and minor Portuguese spheres of influence were carved out of the adjacent interior. The Portuguese, however, initially played a minor role in the slave trade, their interest at that point being more acutely in gold. They nonetheless begin to offer a more complete record of trade activities along the coast, and for the first time, the character of slave trading in the region is brought into sharper focus.

It is also from Portuguese accounts that readers can begin to determine a consequent acceleration of Arab, and specifically Omani, involvement in the East African Trade, but also involving Hadrami and Yemeni clans from the southwest of the Arabian Peninsula. Two Ottoman expeditions are noted by the Portuguese, presumably originating from the Levant, for the purpose of visiting the Swahili city of Mombasa to acquire slaves. The 1606 account of Portuguese mariner Gaspar de São Bernardino, recording his observation on the island of Lamu, notes the arrival of "Arab Moors" on regular expeditions to the islands to fill the holds of their dhows with slaves. Other sources make note of relative prices, observing that the cheapest slaves along the east coast were usually to be found on the islands of Pemba or Zanzibar.

The Portuguese, interestingly, during periods of sporadic control of Mombasa, exercised a degree of policing control over the main body of the coast from Mozambique to Somalia and imposed trade restrictions on all commodities as part of an ongoing effort to firm up their control. They also, however, did what they could to prevent the Arab acquisition of slaves, apparently in outrage at the almost immediate corollary of their conversion to Islam, suggesting some degree of missionary preoccupation with the souls of men and women thus transported.

In 1507, the Portuguese occupied the Omani trade center of Muscat, and there they remained for 150 years or so before they were finally expelled during the second half of the 17th century. From that point on, the Sultanate of Oman began to take the lead as the major Arab power in the East African Trade, and alongside this, a domestic agricultural and plantation economy took root in Oman, with the demand for slaves increasing accordingly. The Portuguese were progressively displaced from all of their key positions down the coast, losing first their grip on the islands of Lamu, and then, in the iconic 1696 siege of Fort Jesus, they were ousted from Mombasa.

Much as they strove, the Portuguese never quite succeeded in imposing absolute control over the coast of East Africa, despite their periodic occupation of all the major ports and fortifications. In 1503 or 1504, soon after their arrival in the region, they seized control of the island of Zanzibar and held on to it as an administrative post for almost two centuries. This, however, did not translate into full control of trade and commerce, which remained substantively in Arab and Swahili hands. In fact, with their loss of Mombasa and an increasingly aggressive pressure exerted by the Omanis in the north, it was only a matter of time before the Portuguese would be obliged to retreat further south still, and in the end, control of Zanzibar passed to the Arabs.

Even a superficial glance at the map of Africa will confirm the natural strategic position of the island of Zanzibar. Situated less than 30 miles from the mainland and at some 950 square miles in area, it is large enough to host a sizable permanent population, and with a natural port and a fertile and well-watered hinterland, its attributes to any power desiring a commanding position over trade with the interior are obvious. Prior to the Portuguese occupation, the settlement lay under no specific authority and developed as what might perhaps be described as an international free trade zone. The Portuguese, considerably more aggressive and better armed than a sundry corps of traders, assumed control relatively easily and maintained that control without difficulty, as they did both the island of Pemba and the coastal port of Mombasa. The rise of the Imams of Oman, a new and forceful power in the theatre, toppled the Portuguese, pushing them southward towards their stronghold of the future Mozambique and their northernmost fortified settlement on the Ilha de Moçambique, a small island situated just a few hundred yards across a shallow strait from the mainland, where a fort had been built and where the Portuguese position in East Africa would be headquartered for another two centuries.

A 19th century depiction of a Zanj slave gang in Zanzibar

SLAVERS REVENGING THEIR LOSSES.

A 19th century depiction of a slave caravan in Mozambique

It was from here, incidentally, that the Zambezi River trade was controlled, and from the early 16th century onward, this remained securely in Portuguese hands. This trade was general, centered on gold, but it diversified into the trade in slaves as the pace of that trade accelerated toward the end of the 17th and beginning of the 18th centuries. The Portuguese style of administration and trade was ad hoc and somewhat fluid, but in general it was factored by a class of trader barons known as Praziero, granted sweeping rights by the Portuguese crown and in time emerging as de facto kings and chiefs, often, like the Arabs, having assimilated to the extent that they were barely recognizable as non-African.

Meanwhile, with Omani control of Zanzibar came a rapid development of trade and administrative institutions, and before long, all the major trade networks up the entire Swahili Coast lay under control from Muscat, with satellite administrations established at each point. Thereafter, all branches of trade along the coast began to accelerate quickly, including, of course, the allied trades in ivory and slaves. The line of demarcation between Arab and Portuguese interests was now drawn broadly at the Rovuma River, today the frontier between Tanzania and Mozambique, and although the Portuguese did periodically venture north on adventures of conquest, for the most part the situation remained static until a later period of European colonization began during the 1880s.

The departure of the Portuguese from the Swahili coast also obscured what had, for a while, been a reasonably clear historic record. Thereafter, only through periodic European accounts can the development of a sophisticated trading economy in Zanzibar be plotted. A slave market was established alongside more general central exchanges, and institutions of taxation and finance were established. The latter involved a large expatriate Indian community, and the intertwining of trade and familial interests between Zanzibar and the west coast of India soon became an established feature of East African commerce. The acquisition of slaves from the interior of East Africa began to supersede acquisitions from Madagascar, and eventually, that branch of the trade disappeared altogether. Around the end of the 17th century and the beginning of the 18th century, an extensive trade in slaves began to center in and around the settlement of Kilwa, an ancient sultanate now subordinated to Zanzibar, from where Swahili and Yao traffickers supplied the coastal trade.

The Yao, were, as they remain today, a large Bantu language group located across what would today be northern Mozambique and southern Tanzania. Like the Swahili, they fell incrementally under Arab influence, and adopting Islam as their dominant religion and trade as their principal occupation, they grew to dominate trade along this part of the coast. Ivory and slaves, of course, formed the basis of this trade, although the Yao tended to place a greater emphasis on slaves than other commodities, and their internal organization reflected this fact. They were significantly more aggressive than the Swahili, and they monopolized a large area associated with the northern quarter of modern Mozambique and the southern reaches of Lake Nyasa. Their market was also somewhat more diversified insofar as they were ideally positioned to ship slaves overland to the Swahili Coast or to Portuguese traders and factors located on the lower reaches of the Zambezi.

Both the Swahili and the Yao, thanks to their mutual adoption of Arab styles of dress and religion, appeared superficially similar and were regarded by both Portuguese and other early European explorers as "Arab". Frequent references made in the accounts of explorers such as Livingstone of "Arab" slave traders typically refer to either the Yao or Swahili middlemen who prosecuted the unpleasant practicalities of the interior trade. Much of the violence, wastage, and horror that Livingstone recorded as his journeys brought him into direct contact with slaving activities derived from the activities of both groups.

As the 18th century progressed and as the pace of demand for slaves steadily quickened, the interior regions affected steadily grew. Financed from Zanzibar and under the control of a small and wealthy Arab/Indian trading elite, private armies were dispatched across an ever-widening region of the East African interior. The simple mechanics of the trade, depending on the power dynamics of any given region, saw either the direct assault of slave-hunting parties on scattered villages and settlements or the simple purchase of slaves from dominant tribes undertaking this work on contract or as a corollary of war and other inter-tribal conflicts. Those individuals that survived the experience of transport to the coast were shipped across the straits to Zanzibar, where they were processed and taxed, after which they were fattened up and generally conditioned for onward consignment. In many instances, young boys were exported as eunuchs and women as concubines, but more frequently for the simple rigors of agricultural labor.

A small number of boys were retained at the coast, and these were inducted into the ranks of the Ruga-Ruga. Ruga-Ruga is a broad umbrella term that was used to describe a general mercenary force applied to a variety of different uses, but in this case to form the offensive front line of slaving militias, who by the end of the last quarter of the 18th century had developed a most fearful reputation. Much of the popular memory of violence and terror still associated with the slave trade in East Africa is attributable to these roving bands of hired killers, under the order of "Arab" warlords and consigned to the business of gathering slaves and, having gathered them, keeping them under control.

Meanwhile, Omani control of Zanzibar was consolidated when, sometime between 1832 and 1840, the Omani ruler, Said bin Sultan, established his seat of authority in the Stone Town of Zanzibar City. By then the Indian Ocean Slave Trade had grown beyond the mere supply of slaves to the markets of Arabia and Mesopotamia and now included the French plantation islands of the Indian Ocean and rogue European traders evading the Royal Navy blockades of the Atlantic seaboard. This marked the point at which the East African Slave Trade began to assume parallel dimensions to the now outlawed Atlantic trade, with similar levels of despoilment, depopulation, displacement, and social disintegration. Added to this was a vastly expanding market for ivory in the industrializing centers of Europe and the United States, and the conditions for a massive humanitarian crisis began to fall into place. By the late 1850s, as Livingstone entered upon the stage of East/Central Africa, this was indeed the evolving situation.

The Universities Mission to Central Africa

"Cannot the love of Christ carry the missionary where the slave trade carries the trader? I shall open up a path into the interior, or perish." – Dr. Livingstone

The Zambezi Expedition arrived at its destination in the autumn of 1858 and encountered immediately a sandbar across the mouth of the Zambezi that inhibited the depth of draft of any boat attempting to enter it. This had not been anticipated, and some private concern was expressed by the staff of the expedition as equipment and materiel were laboriously ferried by whalers from the anchored HMS *Pearl* and the expedition steamer assembled on the south bank of the river in readiness for the journey upstream. By increments, the expedition limped from one sandbar to another, with speculation now beginning to develop regarding Livingstone's state of mind when he declared the river navigable.

Matters came to a head some 250 miles upstream, a little under half the projected distance to Victoria Falls, at that wide bend in the river that Livingstone, in his hurry to reach the coast and make public his discovery, had neglected to explore. Here lay the mighty Kebrabasa Rapids, a

30-mile stretch of white water, now submerged under the Carbora Basa Dam, upstream of which no watercraft of any sort had a hope of passing.

Livingstone's leadership of the expedition was immediately brought into question, and matters hovered in precarious balance until Livingstone, his faith in the providence of his maker unshaken, declared simply that this was a message from God. Clearly, the work of the mission lay not on the Zambezi, but elsewhere, and Livingstone recalled a large tributary flowing into the Zambezi from the north, some way back down river, and this, he declared, the expedition would now explore. The Zambezi was abandoned, and the entire enterprise diverted back downstream and up the Shiré River. A few weeks later, to Livingstone's inexpressible relief, the expedition was delivered to the southern tip of Lake Nyasa, the future Lake Malawi, and a geographic discovery of monumental significance was recorded.

Livingstone's reputation was salvaged, or perhaps, as he would have it, it was simply that his faith had been vindicated. Either way, what remained was to identify a field of endeavor for the Universities Mission to Central Africa, due shortly to arrive off the coast and expecting, as had everyone else, to journey up the Zambezi River to bring civilization to the savages. For this Livingstone chose the picturesque and populated Shiré Highlands, appended to the southern end of the lake and apparently, at least according to him, chosen by God for the ministrations of His faithful.

What Livingstone was apt to ignore, however, in his urgent desire to rescue an expedition under threat from a skeptical board of sponsors unnerved by such an obvious and early blunder, were signs among the peaceful valleys and hillsides of the highlands of fear. Rumors reached him of some unnamed terror moving eastward from the coast, but this was not news that he wished to hear at that moment. He determined, despite the obvious warnings, that this was God's intended field for the UMCA to labor within, and with that conviction, he hurried back downstream to meet the vanguard of the mission as it anchored at the mouth of the Zambezi River.

The mission was led by an Anglican bishop by the name of Charles Frederick Mackenzie. Mackenzie was a man in his mid-thirties, of powerful build, and described by his peers as swashbuckling, suggesting an aggressive approach to his missionary work that perhaps boded well under the circumstances. He was no doubt mollified by Livingstone's optimistic projections, and as the expedition steamer slowly made its way upstream, he was entertained by Livingstone's descriptions of a green and pleasant land and of peaceful and prosperous natives residing in shameful ignorance in a land of God's creation.

As the river steamer arrived alongside the Shiré Highlands, however, and as the mission party disembarked, smoke was clearly visible on the far horizon, and tales of raiding parties of Yao slave traders were now impossible for Livingstone or Mackenzie to ignore. Nonetheless, the mission party set off, with Livingstone in the lead and behind him Bishop Charles Mackenzie, in one hand carrying his bishop's crozier and in the other a loaded shotgun. The irony of this has been observed by a great many subsequent chroniclers and historians, and one can certainly imagine that the irony of it was not lost on either Livingstone or Bishop Mackenzie. The mission party consisted of Bishop Mackenzie himself, several European lay and clerical members, and several armed native levies recruited in Cape Town, numbering among them one or two freed slaves. In addition to this, Livingstone's entourage added more armed men, and overall the party was well provisioned and stoutly defended.

After a day or two of cautious travel among scattered and nervous tribes, known collectively as Mang'anja, news reached the missionaries of a large party of Yao slave traders and their captives moving in their direction. When the two parties met, it marked something of a defining moment in the long history of the East African Slave Trade, the moment that the forces of God and humanity confronted for the first time direct evidence of the despised slave trade. The sight of several hundred captured souls, bound together by goree sticks and on their way to a slave market at the coast, brought into sharp and immediate focus the practicalities of what was taking place.[1]

The missionaries were, of course, motivated to react immediately, and certainly those among the native levies (baptized men who had once been slaves themselves) were extremely agitated and eager to act, and moreover, they were sufficiently well armed to do so. Livingstone, however, counseled caution. He had been in-country far longer than they, and he was sensible to the immediate risks and responsibilities that would accrue from any untoward action. The matter was not quite so clear-cut as it might seem, and there were deeper considerations at play than simply the outrage of Christian soldiers at this manifest display of a reviled trade.

Moreover, slavery as an institution, and the trade in slaves in East Africa, were not at that moment illegal. Although the international trade in slaves was well on its way toward eradication, there were a great many pockets of the world where resistance to abolition was vigorous, and East Africa was one such place. The British, overall, were leading the global abolition effort, and British international influence in this regard was robust, but over East Africa, Her Majesty's government was required to tread with unusual caution. British diplomacy in the western Indian Ocean was at that time both delicate and complicated, and this was because it affected one of the most important British overseas assets, India, over which the British were often guilty of determined tunnel vision.

In brief, the British arrived at a position of nominal dominance in India only after decades, and indeed centuries of maneuver and manipulation against competing Portuguese, Dutch, and most importantly, French interests. One result of the many wars fought between the French and the

---

[1] *Goree Sticks* were devices used to restrain slaves in transit. They consisted of a heavy forked bough cut from a tree, often joined with another to provide a fork at either end, and these were placed over the shoulders of a slave, and an iron pin driven through the leading edges of the fork to bind two slaves together. The name is derived from the island of Goree, associated with the Senegalese city of Dakar, which was, throughout the era of the Atlantic Slave Trade, a major slave depot.

British was the eventual ceding of Indian territory by the French to the British and the firm establishment of Britain as the senior colonizing authority on the Indian subcontinent. In 1857, the British East India Company ceded substantive control of India to the British crown, at which point Queen Victoria became Empress of India and the British Raj was established. This granted Britain an enormous advantage in the region, complementing established British interests in Australia, New Zealand, and the Cape.

To achieve all of this, the British were constrained to acknowledge the authority and power of Omani interests in East Africa and Arab influence generally over much of the western Indian Ocean, the Red Sea, the Arabian Sea, the Gulf of Oman, and the Persian Gulf. The British empire's diplomatic relationship with Oman, although never an easy one, was nonetheless one of the most important of the age and one that would be unlikely to respond well to traditional British gunboat diplomacy. Deeply embedded in the Omani sphere of influence was Zanzibar, and central to the Omani economy was the vast Zanzibari trade hinterland, within which, at that moment, Livingstone and Bishop Mackenzie stood contemplating a slaving party engaged in the prosecution of what was still a legal commercial enterprise.

In the early 1860s, neither the British nor any other European power enjoyed anything other than diplomatic and consular relationships with Zanzibar, since no direct territorial claims had yet been made. Direct European territorial annexation in East Africa and the usurpation of African leadership and rule would not begin to manifest until the 1880s. Although the British consular presence in Zanzibar was certainly of more importance to the Sultan than any other, the Zanzibari trade network was international, and there were certainly other foreign consuls on the island whose competing interests and concerns could not be wholly disregarded by the British. It was, however, the French who worried the British most, and probing French efforts to win trade and territorial concessions from the Sultan of Zanzibar, as well as the French presence on Madagascar and a handful of other islands, were matters of grave concern to the British.

The upshot of it all was that the British were not in a position to impose their abolitionist policies directly on the Sultanate of Zanzibar, and so instead, a delicate and carefully drafted treaty existed that limited but did not outlaw the institution of slavery in East Africa. This was the Moresby Treaty, signed in 1822, which was concerned with the ban on slave trading in British Overseas Territories, in respect of the fact that Britain defined the waters off the west coast of India as British waters. The essence, therefore, of this treaty was to create what was known as the Moresby Line, an imaginary line running from Cape Delgado, at the southern extremity of Zanzibari influence on the East African coast, to a point adjacent to the Indian city of Diu, on the coast of Gujarat. This effectively limited the scope of movement of slave exports out of East Africa to the Red Sea ports, the Arabian Peninsula, and the various territories of the Persian Gulf.

The Moresby Treaty satisfied the British pre-abolition agenda, but after 1838, with the achievement of full abolition, the British began applying more authentic pressure on Zanzibar, as it did on many other of its allies, to effect a comprehensive outlawing of slavery. The Moresby Treaty was followed by the Hammerton Treaty of 1845, brokered by the British Consul on the island, Captain Atkins Hammerton. This document further limited the trade and movement of slaves in the territories controlled by the Sultan strictly to those territories, effectively banning any export of slaves off the African mainland under any circumstances. Slaves could be moved from the mainland to the various islands of Zanzibar, Pemba, and Lamu and there used for domestic agricultural labor, or any other such purpose, but not exported beyond the territorial limitations of the sultanate.

This, of course, was agreed to by Said bin Sultan, the ruling Omani sultan, but it was easily circumvented. Slaves were legally imported onto the island of Zanzibar from the mainland, processed and taxed, and then sold in the central slave market. Thereafter they were legally shipped to Lamu, at the northern extremity of the Sultan's domains, and from there illegally transported the short distance up the coast of Somalia and across the Gulf of Aden. And so, in practical terms, all the careful diplomatic maneuvering that underwrote the Hammerton Treaty amounted to almost nothing in terms of its effect on the slave trade.

Aware of all of this, Livingstone did not feel able to arbitrarily take the law into his own hands and act against the Yao slave traders in any overtly aggressive way. Likewise, at the same time, the Yao slavers themselves, allied to the trade at the coast and subject to the laws of the Zanzibari sultanate, were not in a position to act in any similarly aggressive way towards Livingstone. Livingstone was then a widely known and respected figure, and for him, as a British subject, to be manhandled or injured in the prosecution of his business on the mainland would certainly carry severe ramifications for the perpetrators.

In the end, the slavers decided simply to continue on their way without acknowledging the white men. The resting slaves were roused from their haunches and pressed on along the mountain pathway. At this, Livingstone, at least according to the popular telling of the tale, positioned himself in the path of the leader of the slavers and, placing a hand on his shoulder, commenced praying. Upon this, the slaver fled, with the remainder of his party close on his heels, and the members of the UMCA immediately set to work cutting the captives free. Suddenly, the UMCA found itself in possession of a little under 200 freed slaves, in whose interests it now was not to stray very far from the protection of their liberators.

This established a chain of events that would impact the eventual eradication of the trade, but which would also serve as a sobering lesson for others that would follow in the movement of African humanitarian witness. Bishop Mackenzie thereafter seized the bit between his teeth and took an openly offensive position, with Livingstone somewhat in tow, attacking slave parties and freeing their captives. And bearing in mind that to date, no explanation had been offered to the scattered tribes of the Mang'anja regarding the objectives and intentions of the white men in the Shiré Highlands, the mission soon took on the appearance less of a legation of Christians seeking enlightenment on behalf of the benighted savage and more of an armed intervention force pursuing an aggressive agenda of its own. What this agenda was, few among the Mang'anja could guess, but if logic suggested a local alliance with the missionaries, then that certainly served the short-term interests of a population under pressure.

Livingstone, meanwhile, having delivered the missionaries safely to the field of their endeavor, departed to continue the work of the Zambezi Expedition, which now required a comprehensive geographic survey of Lake Nyasa. He left Mackenzie with both a warning and a stern word of advice. The advice was simply to establish the mission as soon as possible, in order that the word of God might inform some of the actions that had already taken place, and the warning was to avoid at all costs any engagement in local political intrigues.

By then, of course, it was too late, for the missionaries were already deeply embroiled in the politics of a situation they did not altogether understand. They now had under their protection several hundred freed captives who they were morally responsible for, and although they were well supplied with trade goods and could purchase food in good quantity, the burden was not light. But more importantly, Mackenzie now began to field deputations of Mang'anja chiefs who presented him with a difficult conundrum. The missionaries had waged a kind of war against the Yao, a powerful force, and now the Yao were poised to respond against the Mang'anja for bringing against them the white man. It was, therefore, the responsibility of the missionaries to protect the Mang'anja from the Yao by eradicating their presence in the highlands entirely.

This, in effect, would require a war, or at least a battle, and the missionaries had not entered the land to engage in one. Mackenzie had never intended to usurp the secular authority of the territory, and certainly he had never contemplated an alternative regime of law, but the cause and effect of what he had started demanded it, and he had no choice. Leading an assembled force of Mang'anja numbering a little over 1,000 men, supported by the missionary men and guns, a Yao slaving encampment was attacked and razed to the ground. Several hundred captives were released, but utterly exceeded the capacity of the missionaries to care for them and so were subsequently left to fend for themselves.

The Mang'anja chiefs, however, suffering no moral indecision, seized the opportunity and took possession of the captives as the booty of war. The missionaries were forced then to the dispiriting conclusion that they had entirely misinterpreted the dynamics of the situation. All that would appear at that point to separate the Yao from the Mang'anja, as the perpetrators and the victims, was force and internal cohesion. When the tables were turned, the victims manifest themselves as perpetrators with shocking ease. And when the matter was queried, the victorious chiefs simply pointed to the missionaries' own encampment, a protective stockade within which was contained several hundred people already acquired by force of arms and now employed in various tasks, and so, quite clearly, everyone was in the same business.

The moral of the story, therefore, is simply that uninformed action, based on principles of humanity, perceived to be universal, can and often will be usurped by the practicalities of greed, power, and politics. The missionaries had entered the country of their own accord, and with superior weapons and a general attitude of moral superiority, had acted in such a manner as not only to implicate themselves in a crisis, but to amplify that crisis beyond their capacity to control it.

The fates of the Universities Mission to Central Africa and the Zambezi Expedition were effectively sealed. The mission was eventually overwhelmed by events beyond its control, and as it crumbled, its members either abandoned it or died of disease and depletion within an expanding vortex of anarchy and hunger. Bishop Charles Frederick Mackenzie was fated to die a lonely death of malaria on the banks of the Shiré River, and with such a weight of disaster hanging over it, the Zambezi Expedition was eventually recalled. In 1864, Livingstone departed the continent, demoralized and broken, while behind him remained the ever-spiraling centrifuge of death and violence that was the East African Slave Trade.

The Beginning of the End

"I determined never to stop until I had come to the end of my achieved purpose." - Livingstone

In 1864, Livingstone returned to England in disgrace and anonymity. This time no hero's welcome was offered him, and certainly no further sponsorship was made available for him to contemplate a return to Africa. Thus, a curtain fell on the horrors that he had left behind him in central Africa. The fate of the institution of slavery now hung upon the conclusion of the American Civil War, and that faraway suffering that Livingstone had so magnificently publicized with his continental transect a decade earlier was largely forgotten. A few civil servants and a handful of humanitarian and evangelical organizations remained interested in the issue, but for the most part, the affairs of the world continued their orderly procession, and the Sultan of Zanzibar was left to preside over his mercantile empire with little if any interference.

The attention of the Victorian public at that time was captivated by a very public squabble between two luminaries in the exploration field, Sir Richard Burton and John Hanning Speke, over the question of the source of the Nile. Speke claimed that he had discovered it with his exploration of Lake Nyanza Victoria, while Burton maintained that Lake Tanganyika marked the Nile's headwaters. On the evening of September 16, 1864, the two were scheduled to debate the matter, but Speke was killed the previous afternoon by an accidental, self-inflicted gunshot wound while on a hunting excursion. With a touch of the malicious, for which he was well known, Burton suggested that Speke had committed suicide rather than face him in debate, a claim not taken seriously by anyone, but the chain of events nonetheless aided in projecting the question of the Nile to the top of the Victorian geographic agenda.

Burton

Throughout the controversy, Livingstone sought time and again to redirect public attention back to "this open sore of the world," but on every occasion, he was pressed to articulate his own view on the Nile debate. In the end, he realized that if he was ever to return to Africa and reignite public interest in this matter, then he would only do so on the back of a search for the source of the Nile. He accepted a commission from the Royal Geographic Society to extend the search to the south/central watershed, and in 1866 he set sail back to Africa.

At this point, he effectively disappeared from public view. For the next few years, he traveled extensively throughout the southern lakes region, through what would today be modern Tanzania, Zambia, and southern Congo, the legacy of years of tropical disease and manifold disappointments reducing him slowly in mind and body. His journal entries grew increasingly self-searching, depressive, preoccupied with death, and weighed down by a sense of manifest hopelessness. None of this is surprising, for throughout this period he could do nothing but observe and bear witness to the steady reduction of the country through which he traveled to a land of desolation and wandering refugees. He observed and wrote copiously on what he witnessed, and many of these observations make harrowing reading today. "28th July 1867 – Slavery is a great evil wherever I have seen it. A poor old woman and child are among the captives, the boy about three years old seems a mother's pet. His feet are sore from walking in the sun. He was offered for two fathoms [a measure of cloth], and his mother for one fathom; he understood it all, and cried bitterly, clinging to his mother. She had, of course, no power to help him; they were separated at Karungu afterward."

Largely forgotten by his own people, Livingstone was forced to accept the hospitality of these warlords and slave traders, who displayed a duality that Livingstone remarked upon frequently. On the one hand, they displayed a depraved standard of cruelty and brutality towards the Kafir, or the black infidels that they enslaved, and on the other, great kindness and hospitality towards Livingstone. These were often men of great wealth, religious education, and culture, and this dichotomy of behavior consistently amazed Livingstone.

One such man was Hamad bin Muhammad bin Juma bin Rajab el Murjeb, better known by history as Tippu Tip, a nickname that has always been rather enigmatic. Some accounts suggest it as idiomatic Swahili slang meaning simply a wealthy man, and others that it was an onomatopoeic allusion to the crack of rifle fire. Perhaps the most plausible explanation, however, is that Tippu Tip, who was in fact a retiring and somewhat reclusive individual, was afflicted with a nervous tick from which the mocking description Tipoo-tipoo originated.

A portrait of Tippu Tip

Be that as it may, however, Tippu Tip was among the most powerful and ruthless Swahili slave traders of the period, and he commanded a veritable legion of Ruga-Ruga, breaking ground in all directions in the search for slaves and ivory. He was also, in some respects, typical of his caste. Born on the island of Zanzibar around 1832, his father and paternal grandfather were ethnic Swahili, both engaged in trade with the interior and through whom two generations of accumulated wealth was bequeathed upon Tippu Tip. His mother was a full-blood Muscat Arab, which added weight to his lineage, granting him access to the higher echelons of the Zanzibari trade aristocracy. One of the notable architectural relics of the old Zanzibar quarter of Stone Town is the home of Tippu Tip, and notable also is the fact that he was conspicuously pious, a religious scholar, a perfect Arabic linguist, and a man of great social accomplishments.

Didier Tais' picture of Tippu Tip's house

At the same time, he was also what might in modern parlance be described as a warlord. He commanded an ad-hoc army that ran into the thousands, and the hinterland of his influence extended inland from the coast to beyond the continental divide, through the central lakes region, and into the Congo Basin. The irony is that his greatest and most unrepentant critic was Doctor David Livingstone, and yet, in the absence of any meaningful support from home, he was also Livingstone's most dependable sponsor and his guarantor in many perilous regions where the missionary ventured.

Part of this dichotomy of great humanity and great brutality, frequently precedent in religious history, has its roots in the Arabic and Islamic view of slavery, which is an area where the two branches of the slave trade were markedly different. The Atlantic Slave Trade was an industrial and commercial enterprise subject neither to history or sentimentality. In a crude sense, blacks were excluded from the European social charter on the simple grounds of racism and the pre-Darwinian belief that they did not exist in a comparable spiritual state to white Europeans and were thus excluded from the Christian estate. It was not until the Code Noir, or the Black Code, was published in 1685, under the reign of French King Louis XIV, that the soul of the black man was acknowledged by the codification of a series of rules governing the institution of slavery, important among which was a stipulation allowing for induction into the Catholic faith.

With the rise of Islam, however, the institution of slavery, ancient in its application, came under the general thought and law of a faith that found space within its tenets for organized bondage. Islamic law takes account of slave status in a way that Western law, such as it was, did not. Often, Islamic law as it pertained to slaves was intended as an instrument to improve their circumstances, not to mandate its reduction, and often with a view to securing their eventual freedom. It would, therefore, under ideal circumstances, be true to say that, within Islam, slavery existed as part of a finely crafted framework of laws and social conventions that evolved alongside the evolution of Islamic law itself. Islamic law included details as specific as the admissibility of the testimony of a slave in a court of law, the validity of property owned by a slave, the right of a slave to own and bequeath property, the circumstances and conditions of slave marriages, the rights and liberties, if any, of slave progeny, the particulars of punishment under the law applicable to slaves, the relative values of slaves, and, of course, the terms and circumstances of manumission.

And here too lay some of the complexities confronting the practical agents of abolition when dealing with Arab states and Islam. Islamic slavery, for those that chose to view it as such, was relatively humane, and it could not be outlawed at the simple stroke of a pen without interfering with ancient and revered conventions of religion and culture. It was seen often as a cultural practice intrinsic to Arabic society and as opaque to European perceptions as the caste system in India or the practice of Sati, all of which the British approached with extreme caution and always with due regard to avoiding the outrage of foreign sensibilities.[2]

And then there was the additional complication of Western sentimentality. The various levels of diplomatic engagement between Britain, for example, and the many emirates and sultanates of the Arab world, as well as the upper and senior echelons of administration in India, comprised the educated upper and upper-middle class levels of British society. Within this social stratum, there was and had always been an overt admiration and respect for ancient, ruling aristocracies. One need only consider, for example, the career of T.E. Lawrence, or Lawrence of Arabia, for confirmation of this, and certainly the pious, scholarly, and cultured aristocracies of the Arab world tended to excite particular esteem. Add to this a generation of Orientalist artists, writers, poets, and philosophers, borrowing from Napoleon's popularization of oriental themes during his

---

[2] *Sati* – the Hindu tradition of immolation or suicide of a bride at the death of her husband.

occupation of Egypt, glorifying and romanticizing themes of Arabic life, art, lifestyles, and culture. A great many Europeans were apt to observe that the conditions under which a domestic slave in Arabia might live and serve and eventually gain freedom exceeded often the conditions under which white farm, mine, and industrial workers labored in Europe unto death.

A 19th century depiction of a slave market in Egypt

A 19th century engraving of an Arab slave caravan

The horrific experiences of those in bondage in the interior of Africa, those that Livingstone sought to advocate on behalf of, were not always factored into to this perception. Europeans overall tended to see only the improvement wrought upon the life of a naked black savage from the African interior when brought under the light of Islam and civilized accordingly by an association with a superior race. To many such Europeans living, studying, and serving in the various institutions of the East, there was much to admire about the general social order, standards of education, law, and administration under Islam, and very little to be gained by attempting to alter it.

And to risk the collapse of the delicate diplomatic framework that helped keep the British ship afloat in the western Indian Ocean merely to satisfy the pleas of an itinerate missionary in Africa, the occasional braying of a clique of evangelical societies, or aboriginal protection agencies in Britain made absolutely no sense at all. To keep up appearances, however, a small British fleet was maintained in the Gulf of Aden, and a Royal Naval adjudication court was established on the island of Zanzibar to mete out salutary justice in very occasional instances; but beyond that the matter was left well alone, and the Zanzibari and Swahili slave traders were, for the most part, left to get on with their business.

Then, in 1871, a major news story broke, turning the entire situation on its head. The *New York Herald* reported that its roving reporter, a Welsh-American by the name of Henry Morton

Stanley, had discovered the whereabouts of Dr. Livingstone, alive in central Africa. Years had passed since any word of Livingstone had been heard, and the general assumption was that he was dead. His name by then had largely been forgotten, and his crusade had lost all relevance. Stanley, however, who would, on the back of this extraordinary achievement, elbow his way into the top rank of African explorers, published and lectured widely, and the tale that he told was one rich in pathos. He lionized Livingstone, painting a picture of the solitary evangelist, the abandoned moral crusader, set upon his lonely quest to carry the torch of Anglo-Saxon, Christian civilization into the dark heart of Africa. Livingstone's reputation, tarnished deeply by the debacle of the Zambezi Expedition, was suddenly rehabilitated, and a profound sense of shame seemed to settle on the British nation as the tragic fate of this erstwhile national hero was digested.

Stanley

More importantly, perhaps, was the fact that this message was digested not only in Britain, but abroad too, and suddenly the prestige of Victorian Britain hung in the balance. Renewed interest suddenly began to be shown on the issue of slavery in East Africa and the question of abolition. Abolition had taken effect in the United States, and the last frontier of its legal prosecution was East Africa. Quite obviously the Sultan and his henchmen were flagrantly abusing the terms of the Hammerman Treaty, and if the British nation was now poised to set matters right, then surely it was time to bring an end to the institution of slavery in Africa in its entirety.

This surge of sentimentality, however, was not the only force aligning in favor of action against the trade interests of the Zanzibari sultanate. The world was progressing, and a vigorous and aggressive mood of imperialism was beginning to stir in Europe. The independence of Zanzibar was crumbling in the face of the exponentially expanding European spheres of influence. Explorers and missionaries were giving way in Africa to the capital imperialists, who were now shining an ever-brighter light into the dark interior, wherein that great machine of violence and exploitation had for so long churned in anonymity.

Then, further news emerged from Africa. Dr. Livingstone was dead. His heart had been buried among the roots of a baobab tree, and his body brought to the coast by his loyal servants. His coffin arrived in London in the spring of 1874, and he was granted a state funeral. His body was interred in Westminster Abbey, the mausoleum of only the greatest of great British heroes, and a stone placed above it that bore the lines: "All I can add in my solitude, is may heaven's rich blessing come down on anyone, English. American or Turk, who can help heal this open sore of the world."

Abolition

"The slaves in Africa, I suppose, are nearly in the proportion of three to one to the freemen. They claim no reward for their services except food and clothing, and are treated with kindness or severity, according to the good or bad disposition of their masters. Custom, however, has established certain rules with regard to the treatment of slaves, which it is thought dishonourable to violate. Thus the domestic slaves, or such as are born in a man's own house, are treated with more lenity than those which are purchased with money. ... But these restrictions on the power of the master extend not to the care of prisoners taken in war, nor to that of slaves purchased with money. All these unfortunate beings are considered as strangers and foreigners, who have no right to the protection of the law, and may be treated with severity, or sold to a stranger, according to the pleasure of their owners." Mungo Park, "Travels in the Interior of Africa"

In 1872, the decision was made to dispatch a special envoy to the island of Zanzibar tasked with negotiating an end to East African slavery. The man chosen to undertake this task was an imperialist of entirely contrasting character to Livingstone. Sir Bartle Frere, ex-Governor of Bombay and a member of the Council of India, was a man with the establishment interest always foremost in his mind. He was somewhat typical of the British ruling classes at that time, lacking perhaps in subtlety and creativity, but empowered by the mighty weight of the British Empire. The sultanates of Oman and Zanzibar were growing anachronistic, and the ugly little business of slavery in the interior of Africa was now not only a moral affront to the British but an inconvenience. Frere's orders, handed to him personally by the Secretary of State for Foreign Affairs, Lord Granville, required of him to express the disappointment of Her Majesty's government at the lack of effective enforcement of the Hammerton Treaty and to invite the Sultan to cooperate with the British Government in bringing about a final end to the trade in slaves in his domains.

Frere

On January 12, 1873, Sir Bartle Frere steamed into the Zanzibar harbor aboard the Royal Navy yacht *Enchantress*, and initially, amid enormous pomp and ceremony, the way ahead seemed clear. Frere visited the palace of the Sultan, and the Sultan visited the Enchantress, after which negotiations devolved to intermediaries. Needless to say, the Sultan Saleh Bargash Al Menhali, better known as Bargash, prevaricated. His plea was that absolute abolition would destroy the plantation economy of Zanzibar, and that slavery was sanctioned under Islamic law. While both points were valid, a more important truth was that the sultanate was implicated in a vast trade network, both in the interior itself and through wider trade, mercantile, and finance links that reached back as far as India. Slavery endured as a very lucrative business, and powerful interests remained engaged in it.

Matters ebbed and flowed for several weeks, with the British Consul acting as the principal intermediary, until, early in February, a formal rejection of any treaty was issued. It was assumed that somehow the French had been implicated in Bargash's final decision, and this is quite probable. In response, however, Sir Bartle Frere merely shrugged and made his way thence to Muscat, where he found the Omani sultanate more pliable. The actions of the Zanzibaris were, in truth, of little consequence by then. Zanzibar Island and its adjacent coast would simply be placed under blockade, after which no offshore movement of slaves would be permitted.

Sir Bartle Frere then drafted a set of instructions to the British Consul in Zanzibar, affirming that any future shipment of slaves from the mainland to Zanzibar should be regarded as piracy, and that the right of Zanzibari subjects to ship their domestic slaves from port to port within the Sultan's dominions would henceforth be withdrawn. All slave markets were to be closed, and an embargo placed on the customs-houses to prevent the passage of slaves in and out of the market, and the Royal Naval squadron attending to the embargo would be placed on high alert.

Confronted by the inevitable, Bargash eventually ratified the treaty, affixing his seal to it on June 5, 1873. A few days later the central slave market of Zanzibar, the last of its kind in the world, was padlocked shut. Although the terms of the treaty were draconian and rigorously enforced, it took many years for the last organized movement of slaves in East Africa to cease. For some time, the coastal blockade simply drove traffickers underground, and an overland route was utilized to transit slaves to Somalia, from where they were shipped across the Gulf of Aden into Arabia. The institution, however, was in decline, and despite its own best efforts and by the dawn of the 1880s, it had effectively disappeared.

In 1890, a British protectorate was extended over Zanzibar, at which point the island became part of the British Empire, and the traditional authority of the sultans ebbed to a point where the office became simply ceremonial. The traditional domains of the Sultanate were now subdividing under the control of various European powers, and before long the British and the Germans had divided East Africa between them, and the last sultan was deposed during the Zanzibar Revolution of 1964.

Perhaps the most ironic legacy of Dr. Livingstone was the fact that what he failed to achieve in life, he achieved in death. The last formal slave transaction recorded in East Africa was by the Portuguese in 1902. Tippu Tip and others who survived the blockade did so based on the ivory trade, perpetuating slavery in the traditional role of portage for ivory to the coast. Slaves were no longer traded as a commodity. In 1890, Tippu Tip retired to his home on Zanzibar Island, where he composed his autobiography and died a rich man in 1905. Henry Morton Stanley went on to forge his place in the pantheon of great African explorers, and Sir Bartle Frere moved on to an appointment as High Commissioner for South Africa, dying a decade after the Zanzibar affair, in 1884.

Online Resources

Other books about African history by Charles River Editors

Other books about the slave trade on Amazon

Further Reading

Anstey, Roger: The Atlantic Slave Trade and British Abolition, 1760–1810. London: Macmillan, 1975. ISBN 0-333-14846-0.

Blackburn, Robin (2011). The American Crucible: Slavery, Emancipation and Human Rights. London & New York: Verso. ISBN 978-1-84467-569-2.

Church Missionary Society (1869). The slave trade of east Africa. London: Church Missionary Society.

Curtin, Philip D.: The Atlantic Slave Trade. University of Wisconsin Press, 1969.

Drescher, Seymour: From Slavery to Freedom: Comparative Studies in the Rise and Fall of Atlantic Slavery. London: Macmillan Press, 1999. ISBN 0-333-73748-2.

Faragher, John Mack; Buhle, Mari Jo; Czitrom, Daniel; Armitage, Susan (2004). Out of Many. Pearson Prentice Hall. p. 54. ISBN 0-13-182431-7.

Gleeson, David T. and Simon Lewis (eds). Ambiguous Anniversary: The Bicentennial of the International Slave Trade Bans (University of South Carolina Press; 2012) 207 pp.

Hall, Gwendolyn Midlo: Slavery and African Ethnicities in the Americas: Restoring the Links. Chapel Hill, N.C.: The University of North Carolina Press, 2006. ISBN 0-8078-2973-0.

Horne, Gerald: The Deepest South: The United States, Brazil, and the African Slave Trade. New York, NY: New York University Press, 2007. ISBN 978-0-8147-3688-3, ISBN 978-0-8147-3689-0.

Klein, Herbert S.: The Atlantic Slave Trade (2nd edn, 2010).

Lindsay, Lisa A. "Captives as Commodities: The Transatlantic Slave Trade". Prentice Hall, 2008. ISBN 978-0-13-194215-8

Meltzer, Milton: Slavery: A World History. New York: Da Capo Press, 1993. ISBN 0-306-80536-7.

Newton, John (1788). Thoughts upon the African Slave Trade. London: J. Buckland and J. Johnson. at Wikisource

Northrup, David: The Atlantic Slave Trade (3rd edn, 2010)

Rediker, Marcus (2007). The Slave Ship: A Human History. New York, NY: Viking Press. ISBN 978-0-670-01823-9.

Reynolds, Edward (1985). Stand the Storm: A History of the Atlantic Slave Trade. London: Allison and Busby.

Rodney, Walter: How Europe Underdeveloped Africa. Washington, D.C.: Howard University Press; Revised edn, 1981. ISBN 0-88258-096-5.

Savage, Elizabeth, ed. (1992). The Human Commodity: Perspectives on the Trans-Saharan Slave Trade. London.

Solow, Barbara (ed.), Slavery and the Rise of the Atlantic System. Cambridge: Cambridge University Press, 1991. ISBN 0-521-40090-2.

Thomas, Hugh: The Slave Trade: The History of the Atlantic Slave Trade 1440–1870. London: Picador, 1997. ISBN 0-330-35437-X.; comprehensive history

Wright, Donald R. "History of Slavery and Africa". Online Encyclopedia.

Free Books by Charles River Editors

We have brand new titles available for free most days of the week. To see which of our titles are currently free, click on this link.

Discounted Books by Charles River Editors

We have titles at a discount price of just 99 cents everyday. To see which of our titles are currently 99 cents, click on this link.

Printed in Great Britain
by Amazon